James Johnston

The Primitive Sabbath Restored by Christ

An historical argument derived from ancient records of China, Egypt, and

other lands

James Johnston

The Primitive Sabbath Restored by Christ
An historical argument derived from ancient records of China, Egypt, and other lands

ISBN/EAN: 9783337243586

Printed in Europe, USA, Canada, Australia, Japan

Cover: Foto ©Lupo / pixelio.de

More available books at **www.hansebooks.com**

THE PRIMITIVE SABBATH
RESTORED BY CHRIST.

AN HISTORICAL ARGUMENT

DERIVED FROM

ANCIENT RECORDS OF CHINA, EGYPT,

AND OTHER LANDS.

BY THE

REV. JAMES JOHNSTON,

ST JAMES' FREE CHURCH, GLASGOW.

"Since we have arrived at this point, to be speaking of the seventh and eighth day, we must briefly call to mind this also, for the eighth day" (our first) " seems properly to be called the seventh, and the seventh, as it appears manifest, the sixth ; and the former to be properly the Sabbath." *Clemens Alexandrinus.*

"This Sabbath, or seventh day's rest, which the holy seed of Noah observed as holy to God, the idolatrous seed consecrated to the sun, their supreme god, and thence called it *Dies Solis—* Sunday " *Theophilus Gale.*

LONDON:
JAMES NISBET & CO., 21 BERNERS STREET.
GLASGOW : T. MURRAY & SON.

MDCCCLXVIII.

G

PREFATORY NOTE.

In putting into circulation the remaining copies of this pamphlet, I beg to call attention to some fresh light which has been thrown on the subject it treats of by recent discoveries in the buried cities of the old, or rather the early world, in the very region where our race was cradled after the flood, at or near the spot where Adam came fresh from his Maker's hand.

We cannot enter upon the arguments for the traces of a Sabbath, as dug up from the ruins of Nineveh and Babylon, and the translations from the records of the still more ancient Accad. (Gen. x. 10.) Those interested will find an article on the subject by the writer, in the Catholic Presbyterian of January, 1881, published by *J. Nisbet & Co.*, Berners Street, London. We may however say in passing, that the evidence thence adduced, adds greatly to the strength of our argument for the pre-mosaic, we may add the Primitive and Divine institution of the Sabbath. Its recurrence, every seventh day—its character, "a day of rest for the heart"—its very name "Sabbattu," are given in a way which leaves little to be desired, when taken in connection with other testimony, so abundantly in our hands from other sources.

The publication of our pamphlet in 1878, led to much learned enquiry in China, especially regarding the day marked by the character "Bit," which I found in the Foh-Kien Imperial Almanac, referred to on p. 12, the origin and meaning of which no Chinese scholar could explain. The most persevering and successful of those who prosecuted the enquiry, was Mr. Wylie, a profound Chinese scholar. He found evidence, which seems to prove, that the week called planetary, had been introduced into China from India, and that the character pronounced " Bit," in Foh-Kien dialect, and " Mih," in the Mandarine, is a *phonetic* used to give the Indian name Mitra from the Persian Mithra, one of the names for the Sun-god, and used to mark the Sun-day.

The discovery in no way invalidates our argument. See this discussed in a condensation of this pamphlet in the March number of the Catholic Presbyterian for 1881. Mr. Wylie expresses his conviction that there are traces of the septenary division of time in China, *long prior to the introduction of the planetary week from India* in the beginning of the Christian era. The following pages give evidence of its existence at a period so remote as to indicate its derivation from independent traditions of a primeval origin. This would account for the Chinese adopting the Indian names, though brought from a foreign country, so contrary to their customs.

I may remark that the theory of a change of the Jewish sabbath, from the seventh to the sixth day of the week, on the depature from Egypt, is not essential to the validity of our argument for the identity of the Christian with the Creation Sabbath. There are other modes of accounting for it.

I have much pleasure in calling attention to a cheap re-issue of the able and learned sermon on " The duty of observing the Christian Sabbath," by the late Dr. Samuel Lee, referred to on p. 43. It is the fullest and ablest argument in favour of the change at the Exodus from Egypt.

NOTE.—In this our first and crude publication, we see many things we would now express otherwise, or leave out, and many errors which we would like to correct, but time and space forbid. We crave the indulgence of our readers.

J. J.

INTRODUCTION.

THE following pages are the result of researches originally made in China, and renewed during the stormy discussion of the "Sabbath Question" in Glasgow two years ago.

Having no desire to enter the lists of controversy, the materials which accumulated on my hand would have been laid aside after the delivery of two evening lectures to my own Congregation, but for the advice of friends who had themselves read and written on the subject, in whose opinion there was quite enough of what was new and important to claim the attention of intelligent friends of Sabbath observance. I do not presume to think that there is any originality in the main design of the argument. It is well known that several of the most learned and orthodox of the Church of England and Puritan divines of the seventeenth century, maintained that the Sabbath was changed at the Exodus from Egypt, and that the Christian Sabbath is now held on the same day as the primitive or patriarchal Sabbath. My chief aim is to establish the latter; as to the former, it is only referred to as subsidiary to my argument.

During the late, as in all previous Sabbath controversies, it has been constantly asserted by men of undoubted talent, occupying the highest position, that the fourth commandment did not apply to us, because we do not keep the seventh, but the first day of the week; that we had no sufficient warrant for this change from the seventh to the first day, and that the only scriptural period for the commencement and close of the Sabbath is the old Jewish division, from sunset to sunset.

The answers given to these bold assertions seemed to me rather feeble, and much less conclusive than they might have been; and I humbly trust a satisfactory reply will be found in the following pamphlet, which aims at fixing the day and hours of Sabbath observance on what seems the testimony of universal history, the light of nature, and the teaching of Scripture.

There is no superstition in such a regard for the very day and hours of "the day which the Lord hath blessed." And it will be found there was divine wisdom in fixing the day and hour for a period of rest which was designed, not for the regulation of the individual, but for public observance. Laws designed only for the private conscience may admit of latitude as respects time and circumstance; those which are designed for national or universal observance must be definite if they are to be beneficial.

Those employers of labour who compensate their servants for partial work on the Sabbath, by giving them an equivalent rest on other days, deserve all credit for their good intentions, but such a custom has only to become general, and our Sabbath will soon be forgotten or neglected. For this necessity amongst employers, so well disposed toward their workers, and we hope toward the observance of the Sabbath, we blame the Christian public more than those who are driven or tempted to resort to such an expedient.

The very limited time at my disposal for historical or antiquarian researches, even for an object so important as establishing the sacred claims of the Sabbath, has been devoted to the discovery and accurate statement of facts, and but little to the form in which they are presented. I do not think that honest and intelligent readers will lose thereby.

May the "Lord of the Sabbath" condescend to own and bless this feeble effort for the maintenance of His holy day; the sign of His covenant, not only to the Jews, but to all the nations of the earth. May the Sabbath of universal peace and goodwill soon be observed in all lands. May the records of its previous existence be the pledge of its future restoration.

CONTENTS.

CONTENTS.

THE PRIMITIVE SABBATH RESTORED
BY CHRIST.

OF the multitudes of devout Christians who, even in these lax times, strictly observe the Sabbath as a day of sacred rest and worship, how many are there who can give a clearly defined and conclusive reason for the change from what is called the last to the first day of the week? Most will refer to the resurrection of Christ and the example of the apostles. Many will prefer to rest it on the authority of the early church, and some may refer us to the necessity of such a day for maintenance of religious life and its benefits to the human race, for which this day is as good as any other, while others cautiously combine them for the greater security; and all will *feel* that they are right in observing the day which has received such universal and long-continued approval as the day of weekly rest.

But if the questions be urged, Why was such a change made? and, Why should the time-hallowed associations of the ancient church be given up? Why were the divine example at creation, the explicit command from Sinai, "The seventh day is the Sabbath," and the special blessing on that last day of the week, to be all set aside, as is generally supposed, by the early church without the authority of a divine *command* expressed in her records, and without any *reasons* being formally assigned for such an important change? To such questions we purpose to give an answer by shewing that the change from the *Jewish* seventh day was only a return to the more venerable and sacred seventh day of the creation week as originally observed by the patriarchs, and most providentially preserved in the historical records of all ancient nations. This day, though really the seventh, is appropriately called the first, being the first of the Jewish week, and as we shall see was regarded as the first in most parts of the world.

To reply to such questions, that all days are alike in God's sight, and that it was of no consequence which was consecrated, is true enough; but it is not a sufficient answer to the question.

God has a sufficient reason for everything he does, though he may not see fit to assign it: and we feel assured that the founder of our religion had a sufficient reason for the change of the day of rest when the original day was of his own appointment: a reason which it is our duty to search for with all diligence, for the satisfaction of our own minds and the discovery of his wisdom. If there was neither an explicit command for a change of the day,—and we read of none,—nor an obvious reason for it,—though none is assigned,—we could not account for the early church adopting the first day in preference to the old Jewish seventh; and when we consider the tenacity with which converted Jews clung to ancient institutions, we are convinced that had the reason for such a change not been of the most conclusive character, the Christian church, of which at first they formed so influential a part, would not have adopted the new day of rest. They could have remembered the resurrection on the seventh, as we now associate the rest of creation with the first. When we find the Jewish converts, for some time, trying to compromise matters by observing both days, we see the sacrifice they made. When we find the change universally adopted, we have strong proof for there having been some obvious and satisfactory reasons for making such a change. It shall be our humble endeavour to discover what that reason was, which will at once account for the Jewish Sabbath being set aside and the following day consecrated in its stead—a reason which will account for the divine selection of that day, and for the church's ready acquiescence in the Saviour's choice, and being fully satisfied with those slight intimations of his will which we find recorded in the New Testament. There are times when the power of putting questions is often greater than the power of answering them. But when questions affecting the authority and character of the Sabbath are freely put, it is the obvious duty of every man who loves the Lord's day, and knows its vast importance for the interests of religion and the welfare of mankind, to do his best to establish its claims on the conscience and reason of mankind.

Those who are fully satisfied in their own minds as to the authority on which they regard the Sabbath as permanently and universally binding, and are content with the reasons usually assigned for a change of the day, may feel no personal need for further evidence. Yet, for the sake of many whose minds are unsettled by recent controversies, and for the sake of the more sincere of the controversialists themselves, it seems of great importance to make some contribution towards the settlement of a much-vexed question, which is important, not only in itself, but in its consequences.

We suppose every intelligent Christian would feel a peculiar interest in the discovery, if it could be conclusively made, that the day which he observes as sacred to rest and worship is the same as that on which our first parents rested and worshipped; that the Christian and creation Sabbath are identical—observed on that same day on which Jehovah rested from his six days' work, and which he blessed and sanctified for the use of man. If we found that our Lord, in rising on the day after the Jewish Sabbath, really rose on the original seventh day, though called the first in reckoning the week by Jewish notation, it would account for that day being chosen for the resurrection and its future commemoration as the Sabbath which was originally "made for man," though, for special reasons, as we shall have cause to believe, it was temporarily changed to another day for the Jewish nation, and now restored to them as it had been preserved for the world when the old partition wall between them and the Gentiles is broken down.

We are aware that such an attempt to identify the Christian with the creation Sabbath has been often made before without success, and that most regard it as, not only incapable of proof, but, as is not unusual in such cases, as not of great importance if established. We not only consider the question of much importance, but ·that it may be answered. We think the wrong method has been pursued, and the proof has been sought in the wrong direction and too far from home; that, in fact, it lay so near our feet that we have overlooked it. We desire to make the attempt; and, as the argument is cumulative, we claim a hearing to the close before the judgment is formed and the inferences are drawn.

Every reader on the Sabbath question is familiar with the arguments for and against the primeval origin of the septenary week; but the fact that one day in seven was regarded as sacred, and that *that day was identical in order of time with the day which we observe as our Christian Sabbath*, and the significance of that fact in its bearing on the primeval origin of the arrangement of time on the change of the day of rest at the commencement of the Christian dispensation, is strangely overlooked or under-estimated. The deepest significance of a septenary division of time lies in the recognition of one day of the seven being marked off from the

rest by a character of sacredness, or honour, or repose, not
accorded to the others, and observed or bearing evidence of
having been at one time observed as a day of rest or worship.
The argument from the sacred character of one day in seven
is generally given up by the more candid or simple advocates of the early origin of the Sabbath, because the evidence for the strict or general observance of the day is not
so conclusive as they think the case demands. If the force of
the argument lay in the actual keeping of one day in seven as
a day of holy rest and religious worship by ancient heathen
nations, they would be right in rejecting any testimony we have
as incomplete and inconclusive; but such consistent and general observance, within the period of authentic history, is
not to be looked for. Long before the historic period, the
world had cast off the true worship of God, and had fallen
into gross idolatry, and both the time and mode of primitive
worship could not fail to be neglected or corrupted according to the prevailing customs of the day. We see even in
our age of the world the extent to which such corruption
and neglect extend in countries professedly Christian. If
we were left to gather the true time and mode of worship
in the Christian dispensation from the literature and customs of our continental neighbours, we would be nearly as
much at a loss as in searching the scanty records of Egypt,
and Greece, and Rome, for evidence of the strict observance
of a primeval Sabbath; our only wonder is, that so much
can be found to prove that one day in seven had *at one time*
been regarded as a day of rest and worship. It is, as we
hope to shew, from the satisfactory nature of the evidence
in favour of such a sacred day, when that evidence is fairly
put, that we are deeply impressed with the conviction that
a special providence has preserved the records of an original
divine institution, which all the corruptions of heathen
worship could no more efface from the early records of
antiquity than could the gross idolatry of our race obliterate
the original knowledge of God from the human conscience.*

Paul could trace that knowledge of God in the imperfect
outline still visible in the depraved heathen of his day, and
could bring the charge of guilt to their consciences by ap-
pealing to the fact that "what may be known of God is
manifest in them," and that "when they knew God they
glorified him not as God." We may say the same of the

---

* By a style of reasoning similar to Whately's "Historical Doubts," it
would be easy to prove that the continental Sabbath had no existence as a
sacred day, and in England that, by act of Parliament, its sacredness is limited
to the hours of divine worship.

primeval Sabbath, of which providence has preserved the
traces so as to be seen and read by the attentive and honest
student of profane history; and the evidence which we pro-
pose to adduce is similiar in its bearing on the *day* for
divine worship to that of natural theology on the being and
attributes of the *object* of worship.

Whether it was generally known by the early church that
the day on which Christ rose from the dead was the same
day which had from time immemorial been marked as a
sacred day by almost all, if not all, ancient nations, or to
what extent, if known, such a fact influenced the early
church in adopting more readily that day for rest and
worship, we do not now inquire. The fact that the day now
called the Christian Sabbath was known to every nation
whose testimony is of material value in regard to such a
question must first be established, and whether this same
day be that which was originally consecrated by God at the
creation, and now restored with a higher glory and significance to its former use, must be the result of a careful
inquiry or cautious inference. First, then, let us establish
the fact that there was one sacred day in seven, of which
a providential record remains in authentic form, and that
this old sacred day corresponds in the order of time with
our present Sabbath.

Our first testimony shall be derived from an unlooked for
quarter; as that from western nations is better known, let
us in the first instance turn to the remote east.

The antagonists of the primeval origin of the Sabbath
have hitherto claimed China as a witness by her silence in
their favour. They have justly and eloquently expatiated
on the importance of such a witness. The undoubted antiquity of that nation; the scrupulous fidelity with which her
historic books and ancient literature are preserved; the care
with which the calendar has been kept from a very remote
date; the entire separation from all external influence,
especially that of western nations; her autonomy and tenacity of old customs, essentially her own: these and many
other reasons make the testimony of Chinese history of
great value in such a question. No man could suppose
that China would borrow any institution from Egyptians,
Jews, or Arabian merchants, who have been erroneously
thought the bearers of the planetary week from the plains
of Chaldea to Central India.

Dr Morrison, in the beginning of our intercourse with that
strange people, tried to account for the Chinese "having no
Sabbath" by supposing that they had separated from the
rest of the world long before the Sabbath was instituted.

His error as a disciple of Paley was natural at that stage of our knowledge, or rather our ignorance, of the country, and arose from looking in vain for any *actual observance* of a Sabbath in the existing usages of the day. Nothing could be more unreasonable than to expect such evidence, and yet even there we shall get a glimpse, if not of the substance of a Sabbath, at least the shadow, which implies a substance. The peculiar value of the testimony of China lies in the fact that the evidence for a Sabbath, at an early period of her history, is so ancient that to the present generation it has no significance until the light of our Scripture history is thrown on it. It lies as a buried relic of the past embalmed in the nation's memory of a venerable antiquity, and preserved with sacred care in her most authentic and authoritative records. The evidence resembles the fossils of geological epochs, silent, but sure witnesses of former existence and life.

We can bring four of these witnesses, each independent of the other, and separately of value, but their cumulative force, as we hope to shew, conclusive proof of a primeval Sabbath, and that on the same day as our Christian day of rest.

The first we shall bring is from the existing customs of the country, but still a mere fossil of a Sabbath. It is found where we would naturally look for it, among such a people, in their funeral rites in honour of the dead; rites prescribed by law, and observed with slight variations all over China with its four hundred millions. On the death of a father the following are the customs observed :—

In front of the wooden tablet bearing the name and titles of the departed, incense tapers are lighted, and the children prostrate themselves before it every morning during the *first seven days;* and for the next *seven weeks*, on each *seventh day*, the same prostrations are performed morning and evening, with offerings to the departed spirit. In some cases of great devotion or display, the daily prostrations are extended to *seven weeks;* and then the *seven times seven* weekly prostrations follow as in ordinary cases. This, to say the least of it, is in striking harmony with the patriarchal custom as described in Gen. l. 10, when Joseph "mourned for his father seven days," the Egyptians not only joining in his expressions of grief, but conforming to a custom which was probably as common with them as the Jews. In Dr Morrison's account of these funeral rites of the Chinese, the resemblance to those of the Egyptians is striking, and can scarcely be a mere accidental coincidence. He informs us in his "View of China," that "during the first seven days they prostrate themselves every morning and evening. After three times seven days, the funeral procession takes place. . . . After interment, they bring back the tablet, and place before it whole roasted pigs, &c., and for seven times seven days present oblations and make prostrations at morning and evening." This makes ten times seven days: the same combination of the numbers *ten* and *seven* which we find in Egyptian funeral rites: Gen. 1. 3, "And the Egyptians mourned for him (Jacob) *threescore and ten days.*"

The second record of a week in China is found in a very ancient cycle of twenty-eight days, named after the twenty-eight constellations, analogous to our twelve signs of the zodiac. This cycle seems to be an attempt to combine the measure of time by the moon with a multiple of the seven days of the week; and so admirably does this fit in with our custom as Christians, that our missionaries have only to tell the converts that the four characters named Fang, Heu, Maou, and Sing stand for the day of rest, and for all time, past, present, and future, they can know from their heathen almanacs the regular recurrence of our Christian Sabbath.

Our third proof is derived from the Chinese classics, which were regarded with reverence as ancient in the days of Confucius, five hundred years anterior to the Christian era. They were edited or compiled by the sage from documents which could be traced back to a period more remote than any records of antiquity. No profane records can claim a descent so venerable and trustworthy. In these sacred classics there are two passages which were given us by the Rev. Dr Legge, the first Chinese scholar of the day, who is now engaged in publishing a magnificent edition and translation of these works. In one passage the words occur, "Seven days complete a revolution"; in the other, "On the seventh day all the passages (*i.e.* public roads and canals) are closed." On these two brief passages the Chinese critics have expended an amount of profound erudition and endless conjecture, which would fill volumes, but without any satisfactory explanation of their meaning. The variety of their theories only shews the insufficiency of any to satisfy or convince. The true import of these sentences had been lost in all likelihood long before the days of Confucius, who, with his usual reverence for what was ancient, put them among the words of their holy men; and there they stand, witnesses, we think, to a primeval revolution of seven days, and a day of rest "when the passages were closed." This seems the only way of accounting for their presence in these books of genuine antiquity and authority.

The fourth testimony is in some respects more striking than even the preceding; and, as we think, clearly pointing to the hands of an overruling providence in preserving the record of a primeval Sabbath, as having been at one time an institution in the everyday life of that peculiar nation, the oldest existing nation in the world. It is found in the imperial almanac of China, which is issued yearly by imperial authority under the editorship of one of the government offices, the Board of Rites. It is regarded as of such importance that it is a penal offence to issue an edition in any part of the empire without the sanction of the emperor. In this almanac there is a particular character found occurring throughout the year on *every seventh day*, and that day is *our Christian Sabbath*. The character employed is not found in common use; the meaning given to it in their dictionaries is "secret" or "closed." How it first got there, or what it indicates in that position, no one can tell. The literary graduate who was appointed by the Emperor or the "Board of Rites," to publish the almanac for the province of Foh Kien in 1854, wrote in answer to a friend of ours, "'The character means secret or closed, but who put it there I never heard. I only know that it has always been there from time immemorial, and must ever continue there." This is characteristic of Chinese conservatism. The ignorance of its import is a proof of the extreme antiquity of the usage. The preservation of what has so long been an unmeaning mark of a particular day, is a proof of the national reverence for everything that is ancient. There the character stands, "secret" or "closed," a mark for our sacred day under the new dispensation. May we not regard it as a happy pledge that China shall yet combine in her weekly customs the dead record of a primeval Sabbath with the living practice of the Christian day of rest. This, as we shall presently see, was the case in Western Asia and Europe, where the record of a Sabbath remained as an unmeaning dead letter until the resurrection of Christ imparted to it significance and vitality.*

We shall not stop now to draw the inference which we might legitimately deduce from the foregoing facts, but shall proceed to point out other interpositions of Providence in the preservation of the historic evidence of the identity of the sacred day among heathen nations with our Christian Sabbath. We shall pass over the testimony of India and other nations of Eastern Asia, although it could be shewn that it is similar in character, if not the same as that of

---

* See Appendix A.

China, but not so conclusive, nor so obviously independent of all external influence. It is admitted on all hands that in Asia, the original seat of the human race after the flood, the traces of a septenary division of time, with a day possessing a character of sacredness or dignity, are clear enough; and it is also admitted the Egyptians preserved a record of this institution even when its only use seemed to be to give names to the days; and its principal day was scarcely distinguished from the others, except by its bearing the name of the sun, as the chief of the heavenly bodies, and the principal deity of most idolatrous nations.*

We do not now discuss the question of its origin, whether primeval or planetary; that we shall treat of further on. We only refer to the fact, admitted even by those who have most ably advocated the later origin of the week and of the Sabbath. The point to which we would now call attention is the introduction of this week into the Roman empire about the commencement of the Christian era, a circumstance which indicates, as we think, providential interposition and peculiar significance. It is admitted by every competent judge of ancient history, in its bearing on the great purposes of God, that the heathen Roman empire was made the unconscious but powerful agent for preparing the way for the ultimate spread and establishment of Christianity; and of the many services she was made to render to civilisation and Christianity, not the least important was the introduction of that division of time which was to be sacredly observed wherever the Christian religion was introduced, a service strangely overlooked or undervalued.

Roman chronology is thankfully acknowledged by the civilized world as a boon, but the benefit rendered in the recognition and establishment of a week of seven days is not so readily admitted, and yet the introduction of the Julian year was not so great a benefit to the church and the world as the introduction of the week.

We do not refer to the edict of Constantine, but to the acts of pagan Rome, the unconscious instrument of an overruling providence. It is the more remarkable that pagan Rome should have introduced a hebdomade into the empire when we know that it was contrary to her old division of time into eight days, and to the classical usage of Greece, her mistress and model in so many things when time was measured in decades. That she should set aside the ancient and honoured customs of Italy and Greece, to adopt the system of the Egyptians, is a strange and significant fact. Such

---

* See important evidence on this subject, Appendix B.

changes in the customs of a people are not easily effected, nor are they attempted by wise rulers without strong motives.

There is some uncertainty as to the exact time and form in which the week was introduced, but it is likely that it was when Julius Cæsar reformed the calendar. That it was derived from Egypt, from which he took the system of chronology, cannot be doubted, as the *names* of the days of the week and the *order* in which the names occur are evidently borrowed from the Egyptian week, but whether introduced at the same time or a little later we cannot be certain.

Dion Cassius, whose position and character as a historian renders his testimony to what came under his own observation and to all the later events of Roman history of the greatest value, informs us that before the death of Adrian, which occurred in A.D. 138, the custom of observing a week of seven days was universal *even in Italy and Greece*. He mentions these countries because the custom was not formerly known, while in other parts of the empire, especially in the east, it was of unknown antiquity.

Now if the customs of these countries had been so far remodelled as to allow the week to be universally observed in 138, the introduction of the system must have been much earlier. We know how tenaciously these old nations cling to the ancient customs. It is not so long since the change from the *old* to the new style could be said to be *universally observed* in our country, although legally adopted in 1752; and if it took nearly a hundred years to bring our *customs* into harmony with the *laws* on so simple and needful a change, it would probably take longer time, or a greater stretch of authority, to get Italy and Greece to change the arrangement of time by which their markets and courts of law, and in fact most of their social and domestic customs were regulated. If, as is probable, the change was effected when the new calendar was introduced in the year 46 B.C. it would be a late enough date to account for the universality of the custom in A.D. 138.

That the change was common in literary circles at a much earlier period is known to the students of history and the historic fact, which Dion records is the only satisfactory account we have seen of the way in which the earliest Christian writers used the old heathen names of the week, and in writing for heathen readers seemed to take for granted that they knew names which are not found in the earlier classics of Greece or Rome, as belonging to seven days of a recognised week. The early apologists, writing to the heathen, use the name Saturday, or the day of Saturn, for the Jewish Sabbath, and Sunday, or day of the Sun, for the day of Christian rest; and what is still more remarkable, they use our designation *the Lord's day*, not as if new or unfamiliar to the heathen, but as a well known name for that day which they at other times call the *day of the sun;* and we find that designation *Lord's day* used by the heathen with no reference to, or knowledge of, Christ or Christian ideas. *The Lord's day* was with them the day on which they worshipped their god Apollo, and in honour of whom the *Sunday,* the Lord's day. It is for this reason that the Emperor Theodosius, in issuing an edict for the better observance of the Christian Sunday, calls it "the *true Lord's day,*" as if the day set apart by their heathen ancestors for the worship of *Baal,* or *The Lord,* of whom the sun was the idolatrous emblem, had now found its proper designation, and its *true* LORD.

The apostle John in the Apocalypse uses the same word (known alike to heathen and Christian), and in doing so by inspiration he consecrated the *name* as the day had been originally consecrated by the resurrection of the Lord Christ. There is no necessity for forming it by analogy from the Lord's supper. That this division of time into weeks with names derived from the seven planets, as being familiar to the Egyptians and most Asiatic nations, was introduced by the Romans at an early period of the Christian era, if not before its commencement, seems to be put beyond a doubt by the way in which Dion Cassius writes of the destruction of Jerusalem, which occurred A.D. 70. In writing of that event, he evidently draws his minute account from the details of contemporary records, or at all events, records made when the facts were fresh in the memory of the writers from whom he derived his material. We learn from these contemporary or recent accounts that the so called planetary week was then in common use amongst the literary men of the *first century.* We are told, for example, that the Jews abstained from aggressive warfare on *Saturday,* a fact which Josephus also records, but gives truly as a reason that it was then *Sabbath,* shewing that the Saturn's day of the heathen and the Sabbath of the Jews were identical. And again, Dion referring to those who took refuge in the temple after the city was taken, he says, "Nor if they had defended it equally on all the days could it have been taken, but because on *Saturn's day,* as they call the day, they refrained from fighting."[*]

But it is needless to multiply proof that the planetary, or, as we would call it, creation week, was introduced into

---

[*] See Appendix C.

the Roman world, and had become a recognised custom at the commencement of the Christian era. We call attention to the fact that it was then, or shortly before, introduced, as Dion Cassius says, as a new custom, in which the devout Christian will see the hand of an over-ruling Providence, rendering the Christian week with its customs more easy of introduction, and preparing the way for the universal establishment of the Christian Sabbath, with all its blessings spiritual and temporal for the church and for the world. This will form our next historic fact, viz., that the sacred day of the week then introduced was the same in order of time with the Christian Sabbath

The fact to which we now call attention is of much greater interest and importance than that to which we have just called attention. The providential introduction of the week of seven days was chiefly of importance from its bearing on the striking coincidence which we shall now point out.

It is not necessary to prove that a week must have one day which stands out distinct from all the others by some peculiar feature of its own; and it would be easy to prove that every division of time corresponding to our week has always had one day of a *sacred* character, whether it be the eight days of the Romans, the nine days of the Peruvians, the seven days of the Jews and of the vast majority of nations in all ages and every quarter of the world. The apparent exceptions are too insignificant to call for notice here.

It will be found that it is this sacred-day which originates and gives significance to the week. It forms its consummation or its commencement, and without it a week would have little import or use; even when one day of the week has been devoted to pleasure it will be found that it is the perversion of a sacred day. The world's septenary *holidays* are derived from the church's *holy days*.

Even in the planetary week, about which we shall have something to say by and by, there is one day marked off as distinct from all the rest—a day as much distinguished from all the other days as the sun is distinguished from the planetary bodies. The *Sunday* was always regarded as sacred to the supreme deity of every heathen nation, and both the day and the deity were looked upon as being superior to other days and other gods, as the sun is superior to the moon and the five visible planets. It was this we doubt not that led to that day on which the sun, or god of the sun, was worshipped being called the *Lord's day* (η κυριακη), our Saxon designation being the literal rendering of both the Greek and Latin, as theirs was the translation of Baal, the title by which the sun-god was worshipped in the original seat of the human family, and the source of the idolatrous worship of the East, if not of the world. We hope to shew before we close that while the names of the days of the week were derived from the planetary bodies, the week itself is not derived from them, and though perverted to heathen worship, they are no more heathen in their origin than those heavenly bodies which have been made the abodes or representatives of imaginary deities; that, in fact, the careful student of history will allow, the week is no more derived from the planets than the planets from the week. The sacredness of this Sunday varied in different lands and different periods, according to the religion and religious character of each age and people.

Not only was this one day in seven, which was also the Sunday, regarded as a sacred day, but the interesting fact to which we now call attention is that this day was the day on which our Lord arose from the dead, and which was henceforth kept by the Christian church as the day of rest. The Christian sacred day, called, in its relation to the Jewish Sabbath, the *first day* of the week, coincided with the heathen sacred day, the "venerable *day of the sun.*" This could be no casual or unimportant coincidence; we must recognise some significant purpose in it. Christ, as Lord of the Sabbath, could, if he chose, have consecrated any day of the seven; and when we see the arrangement of his death and burial with the three days of predicted rest in the tomb made to coincide with a resurrection on this day,—which had been preserved by sacred tradition and earliest custom as a holy day, not by the Jews, or merely by some insignificant notion, but sanctioned, as we have seen, by the whole world, with trifling exceptions, and introduced about the same time into that powerful and enlightened monarchy which had been the divinely appointed means for preparing the way of the Lord,—we are constrained to recognise the hand of a special providence. It cannot, of course, be supposed that the heathen adopted the Christian day; they had known it long before the Christian era, and were in no humour to adopt Christian customs. As little can it be supposed that our Lord did any honour to a heathen custom; there must be some deeper and holier cause for such a striking coincidence. Before we consider the source of this coincidence of the sacred day in the Christian Church and the heathen world, let us give conclusive proof that it is an historic fact, and not a mere fancy. Justin Martyr puts it beyond a doubt in his dialogue with Trypho the Jew. "He carefully distinguishes Saturday as the day after which our Lord was crucified from Sunday upon which he rose from the dead."*

Here we learn two facts; first, that *Saturday* was the day after our Lord was crucified, and consequently corresponded with the Jewish Sabbath. This is in harmony with what we learn from Porphyry, who says that the Syrophenicians observed the same sacred day as the Jews, and we know that Saturn, not Apollo, was their national god. Second, we see that the day after Saturday, on which our Lord arose from the dead, was *the day of the sun.*

Eusebius says, "Constantine commanded his army dilligently to honour the salutary day which happens to derive its name from the lights and from the sun."† This was when legislating for the better observance of the Sabbath, and Clemens Alexandrinus speaks of the origin of the name the *Lord's* day as being derived from light, being named after the sun; and identifies the old planetary Sunday and the Christian Sabbath. "In regard we on that day received the knowledge of the truth by the Holy Spirit, who fell upon the faithful in the form of fire," Strom., b. vi. Pentecost, as we know, fell on a Sunday that year.

Eusebius in his oration in praise of Constantine says that the Emperor commanded his army to worship God on "a fit day;" and it is worthy of notice that while he gave different directions to the Christians and the heathens of which it was composed, he commands both to worship on the same "fit" day which in each case designates the *sun day* or *Lord's day*, which are used as convertible terms. His words are, "But to them that as yet have not embraced the doctrine of the divine faith, he issued out a precept in a sacred law, that on *Sundays* they should go out into a pure field in the suburbs, when, after a signal given, they should together pour forth a prayer to God which they had learned before." In another passage he quotes the words of Constantine's exhortation to the army to pray on "that day which is chief and first of other days, and which is truly the Lord's (κυριακη) day, and the salutary day, and which derived its name from light, life, immortality, and everything that is good." But we need not multiply passages to prove that the Sunday of the planetary week coincided with the day of Christ's resurrection, and from that date the Sabbath of the church of all lands and all future ages.

Before inquiring whether this identity necessarily implies that it is also the original day of rest instituted by God at

---

* See Smith's Bib. Dic.   † Life of Constantine.

creation,—not a mere accidental coincidence, but a deeply significant providential circumstance,—it will be desirable to inquire briefly whether the hebdomadal division of time be of planetary, and consequently heathen or human origin, or be a primeval divine institution.

We can only spare time for a few considerations which will, we trust, after what we have already proved, be sufficient to carry conviction to candid inquirers, in favour of the divine origin of the week and of the Sabbath.

I. We would observe that the naming of the days of the week after the seven planetary bodies is in itself no proof that the division of time into weeks was not long anterior to the practice of imposing names on the separate days. It is not Quakers only who can dispense with names. The Jews used no names for any day save the Sabbath, probably because the custom of naming the days had not been introduced and at a later date, or if customary when they left Egypt, because the custom and the names were alike heathen. Still it was a natural and convenient device which can be easily accounted for from the coincidence of number, and would be the more easily accounted for when idolatry had corrupted the true religion. It would give a colour of truth to the false religion to note such a harmony between the objects of Sabean worship and the number of days originally instituted by God. It seems impossible to *prove* more than a mere coincidence. It is admitted that there is no historical evidence of this having been the *origin* of the week; the only authors who speak of its planetary origin are all avowedly of later date. The week can be proved, and is indeed admitted, to have existed, and the names imposed, long before any record of the theory can be discovered.

II. We know that it was a very common practice to trace many things to the heavenly bodies which science and reason have long discovered to have no connection with them. The metals and the seven sounds in music were long regarded as mysteriously connected * with, if not derived from, the seven planets. The evidence for the general belief of this by the ancients is much stronger, and that it took a far firmer hold of the minds of philosophers than the planetary origin of the week. Dion Cassius gives it only as *a theory*, not as an ascertained fact. Surely candour and common sense should lead men in these days to reject the theory of the planetary origin of the week when we have universally

---

* See Appendix D.

set aside the pretty and equally plausible notion of the
" music of the spheres."

III. The coincidence of the number of days, and of the
planetary bodies, has the appearance of *being forced* or ac-
commodated. The classing of the sun and moon, so different
in appearance and motion from the five planets with which
they are classed, looks like an adaptation, and seems rather
to be an attempt to make the heavenly bodies harmonise
with the number of days previously fixed than of fixing the
number of the days by the number of the planets.

IV. If the *naming* of the days after the heavenly bodies
be idolatrous, as it seems to be, even that custom, taken in
connection with its forced character, appears to point to an
institution of a sacred day. That day named after the sun
was either previously regarded as different from the rest, or
in future would be regarded as having a place of pre-emi-
nence. History shews that it was so regarded as consecrated
to the supreme deity; and we can scarcely suppose that
idolaters were the first to set apart a day for rest or sacred
uses. Natural religion would be likely to suggest it from
the earliest time, even if God had not appointed it. This,
however, may be disputed, and we do not build upon it.

V. We find that the week of seven days, with one day of
rest, has existed where there is not the remotest reference
to the seven planets in connection with it. In China the
most independent and important witness that can be ap-
pealed to, the week is in the nearest approximation to the
month, and the days are named after the twenty-eight constellations—purely arbitrary signs from grouping the stars from
fanciful resemblances; as in our western signs of the zodiac—
the girl, the ox, the tail, the heart, the stomach, a sieve, &c.
This testimony is of great value from the attention paid to
astronomy and chronology by the Chinese from earliest
times, and from the accuracy and extent of their knowledge.

VI. The testimony of those nations in which we find a
different division of time along with a sacred day, is strong
evidence against the planetary origin of the week, so that ten,
nine, and eight days of Greece, and South America, and Italy
are all turned as evidence against the planetary theory. They
seem to prove that man feels the need, and has a recollection
of a day of rest or worship, while natural religion fails to give
uniformity in the time of its recurrence. Men may corrupt
the practice and change the day from a seventh, to an eighth,
ninth, or tenth, but the original idea is there—God's witness
in favour of that tribute which is due from the creature to
the Creator. This will be seen more fully ere we close.

VII. We may observe that the testimony from Greek and

Roman literature in regard to the week and a day of rest is comparatively of little importance. Compared with the records of Egypt and the East, and especially of China, it is of little significance on subjects of real antiquity. These are comparatively modern nations; and while they evidently borrow their religious systems from the East, they as evidently alter and corrupt them, or we may say, idealise and rationalise them. That they should have altered an old tradition of a *seven* day week to one of eight or ten days, is not to be wondered at. It rather confirms the uniform testimony of three-fourths or nine-tenths of all the nations of antiquity in favour of a week of seven days. It shews that *seven* is not a natural number which men would necessarily or generally have fixed on of themselves. It stamps the will and authority of an early legislator on the arbitrary number *seven*. Rationalism would prefer the number *ten*, as we see in Greece and France at the Revolution.

VIII. It is an important admission, drawn, or rather forced, from the opponents of a primeval Sabbath, that the origin of the week can be traced to the first seat of the human race after the flood. Mr Hessey refers to this in trying to account for the wide diffusion of what he calls the planetary week. But is it not far more confirmatory of its primeval institution by divine authority? It is just the quarter from which we would expect it to emanate. It is as far back as we can go by the imperfect help of profane history; and if we take into account the very probable opinion that the Chinese emigrated to the far east before the race had fallen into idolatry, as the history and old patriarchal customs of that ancient people seem to prove, it makes it most probable, we might say almost certain, that the planetary names were not imposed until a later period, and after the rise of Sabean worship.

IX. Add to these considerations, and many others that could be named, the simple record of the book of Genesis, as to the origin of the week and the Sabbath,—see how it fits into all the facts of history in all parts of the world,—and can any reasonable man doubt that it is the true account of the origin of both. To deny it is to reject the sure record of inspiration, to oppose the testimony of history, to resist the inference of reason, and to doubt the beneficence of the Creator in his original plans for the temporal and spiritual welfare of his creatures.

We have always felt that far too great a value was set on the references in the classics by both friends and opponents of the antiquity of the Sabbath. In *questions of evidence* the nearer we come to the time any event took place the more

B

reliable will it be if the witnesses possess ordinary intelligence and honesty. The evidence we have on this subject
in the classics is all at second hand, or too recent to be of
much use.

The wisdom and culture, the grace and fancy, the social,
political, and intellectual superiority of the Greeks and
Romans, are of no account in a mere question of evidence,
however important in a matter of taste or opinion. The
most conclusive proof of the secondary value of the testimony of classic notions as to the true week and sacred day
is found in the practical acknowledgment of classic notions
themselves. Whenever the Romans came into direct contact
with the ancient chronology of the Egyptians they at once
saw and admitted its superiority; and the first and greatest
of her emperors inaugurated a new era by adopting it and
making the system of a despised and conquered province the
rule for the greatest empire of the world, a system which
continues, with slight modification, the best to this present
time; and as we have seen, in adopting the chronology
they adopted at the same time, or a little later, the Egyptian week with the sacred day, also taking the order of the
days as they found them and translating the names into
their own language; a most convincing proof of their esti-
mate of the vast superiority of the ancient Egyptians
over the bungling Roman measure of time by weeks and
years.

We have made frequent reference to one day in the week
as being of a sacred character. This day, as we have seen,
was not actually observed as a day of rest or worship within
the historic period, but the idea of its true character was
preserved in almost all parts of the world, whether right
division of time were preserved or not. In China we saw
that the idea of rest was preserved in their sacred books,
and the practice of worship is still kept up in their funeral
rites on a seventh day, and the worship of ancestors is the
principal part of the popular religion. In all those countries
in which the planetary week prevailed, the *Sunday* is consecrated to the worship of the principal deity. In India and the
surrounding countries the same rule nominally holds good,
while in Ceylon, to which the Budhists were driven, carrying
with them some of the oldest traditions of the continent, the
custom prevails. Hardy informs us that there are four
days in each month called "poya," on which "great merit
is obtained by laymen observing the precepts" of their religion. "These days must be observed with clean garments
and clean hearts. They must prepare their food for that
day the day before. They must not trade nor even calculate

the profits of trade. They must do nothing that will injure another. They must recite the precepts and meditate on the impermanency, sorrow, and mutability connected with all things."* In South America we learn from Bailly, quoting from Garalasso, that "according to an ancient law of the Inca Pachacutee there ought to be in each month three days for festivals and markets, and that the people were to work eight days and rest on the ninth." †

The fishermen, a race amongst whom old superstitions and traditions cling long, still refrain from fishing on the ninth day in some parts of the southern continent.

This idea of the sacredness of a portion of time to rest and worship is clearly brought out in the laws and customs of the Romans, though we cannot say that it was kept up at weekly intervals, still less, that it was observed on the intro-duction of the planetary week. On the feriæ or sacred days, to most only holidays, " free born Romans suspended their political transactions and their law-suits, during which their slaves enjoyed a cessation from labour.".‡ " The people generally frequented the temples of the gods, and offered up their prayers and sacrifices." On the more sacred of these days, " the *rex sacrorum* and *flamens* were not even allowed to see any work done; hence, when they went out they were preceded by heralds, who enjoined the people to abstain from work. Those who neglected this admonition were not only liable to a fine, but in case their disobedience were intentional, their crime was considered to be beyond the power of any atonement."§

The preceding quotation recals the strictness of the Mosaic law with its penalty of death to the violater of Sabbath rest. The Romans did not inflict that penalty, but for the wilful transgressor there was *no atonement*, while the unconscious transgressor might atone for his fault by a sacrifice. The following reminds us vividly of the Saviour's commentary on the Jewish law as to what might be lawfully done on the Sabbath :—

"It seems," says Dr L. Schmitz, " that doubts as to what kind of work might be done at public feriæ were not unfrequent; and we have some curious and interesting decisions by Roman pontiffs on this subject. One Umbro declared it to be no violation of the feriæ if a person did such work as had reference to the gods, or was connected with the offering of sacrifice." (The priests in the temple

---

* Hardy's Eastern Monachism, p. 236.
† Humboldt's Researches, v. i., p. 285.
‡ Smith's Classical Dictionary at Feriæ. § Ibid.

profane the Sabbath and are blameless.) "All work, he moreover declared, was allowed which was necessary to supply the urgent wants of life."—*Smith's Dictionary*.

"The Pontiff Scævola, when asked what kind of work might be done on a *dies feriatus* answered that any work might be done if any suffering or injury should be the result of neglect or delay; as for example, if an ox should fall into a pit the owner might employ workmen to lift it out, or if a house threatened to fall down, the inhabitants might take such measures as would prevent it falling without polluting the sacred day."—*Smith's Classical Dictionary*.

These quotations need no comment. So close is the resemblance to the character of a Sabbath, with its rest and worship, and its works of necessity and mercy, that were it not for the absolute impossibility, moral or physical, we would be led to suppose they were taken from the laws of Moses or of Christ. But the primeval Sabbath as described in Genesis sufficiently explains the existence of such ideas wherever the descendants of Adam and of Noah migrated with the deep impressions of a divine command upon their memories, and the divine and patriarchal examples warm in their hearts, and the testimony of conscience, and hopes of the "rest that remaineth" to preserve and practise their religious duties. Is there not in this divinely impressed ideal of a Sabbath, traced in such remote periods and distant regions, and in the preservation of these records of ancient times, the hand of an all-wise over-ruling Providence, telling the whole world that "the Sabbath was made for man at the first?" and may we not hope that all lands are yet destined to enjoy the blessings of that holy rest?

We are now able to see a satisfactory reason for the change of the Sabbath at the resurrection of Christ. It has generally been assumed as an indisputable fact that the Jewish Sabbath was on the original seventh day of creation; and those who have called this in question have not given sufficient evidence to satisfy earnest inquirers that there was a change made at the departure from Egypt; and the historical evidence for the identity of the Christian with the creation rest has not been attended to. In the light of the chain of facts which we have brought forward in favour of this identity, we are prepared to understand those passages which are generally supposed, without any proof, to identify the Jewish Sabbath with the patriarchal. The brief references that are at first made to the Sabbath, after a period of silence extending over so many centuries, need explanation, and it is one mark of the correctness of our theory, that it is not only in harmony with all that is said on the subject, but that it throws light on some things which are otherwise not easily explained.

The passage in Exodus xvi., where the Sabbath is first commanded to the Israelites, has all the appearance of being a command to observe as the future Sabbath of the nation the seventh day *from the fall of manna.* We cannot otherwise understand why an explicit command should be required at that stage of the nation's history. It would not have been required if there had been no change of the day, for both Israelites and Egyptians had a knowledge of it. A command to observe it more in harmony with its original institution might have been necessary, but not as we find it, a command to consecrate each seventh day, unless we assume that the blessing recorded in Gen. iii. 2, was proleptical, and even the planetary week of later origin. If there was a change of the day at the departure from Egypt, it will explain the fact recorded in the first verse of that sixteenth chapter, that the children of Israel made a day's march from Elim to the wilderness of Sin on the fifteenth day of the second month—the day before the fall of the manna, and *which would be a Sabbath* if there had been no change. The manna fell on the 16th, and continued to fall until the morning of the 21st, six days; and the 22d, the seventh day of this heavenly food, was the Sabbath *now commanded.* It would have been a strange introduction to a series of Sabbaths of strict rest when no man was to move out of the camp, either to gather manna or sticks to cook it, if the cloudy pillar had led the whole host on the previous Sabbath a toilsome march from the wells and palms of Elim into an arid region, without any apparent reason of necessity or mercy to justify such toil. It explains the surprise of the "rulers of the congregation" (ver. 22) at the people gathering a double portion, on the sixth day, of manna. They doubtless expected that the supply would stop on the old creation Sabbath, which would have fallen on the 23d, and that the people were to gather the supply for that day on the sixth day of the creation week. But the common people, taking the command of Moses literally, and seeing the larger provision on the *sixth* day of manna, which was only the fifth of the original week, gather a double portion that they may rest on the sixth day of creation week, which is henceforth to be *their* seventh day of rest.*

The reply of Moses is in harmony with this change. In ver. 23 he says, "This is that which the Lord hath

---

* See Appendix E.

said, *To-morrow* is the rest of the holy Sabbath unto the Lord."

Such a change might have been expected at the commencement of the peculiar and temporary economy of the Jews. It was desirable to break loose from all the idolatrous customs which the people were apt to associate with the sacred day from the Egyptian mode of observing the Sabbath. We find other changes of a similar kind in principle to make a distinction between the Israelites and all the idolatrous nations around them.

It throws light on the fourth commandment itself, and renders its grave argument more binding on us than on the Jews. While the fundamental command, "six days shalt thou labour," &c., "but the seventh is the Sabbath," is equally applicable whatever day be regarded as the first of the series. The argument from God's example of resting on the seventh day after the six days work of creation is specially applicable to us if the day we so observe is indeed the very day on which Jehovah rested; and it shews the striking propriety of Moses's argument in Deut. v. 15, where the law is repeated, not from Sinai by the voice of God, but as explained and enforced by a wise ruler, who is also the teacher of the peculiar people. He there urges obedience to the fourth commandment, not as in the tables of stone, which was the form adopted for all nations,—"For in six days the Lord made heaven and earth, and rested the seventh day," &c.,—but in an argument which came home to their personal history, " Remember that thou wast a servant in the land of Egypt, and the Lord thy God brought thee out," &c., " therefore the Lord thy God commanded thee to keep the Sabbath day."

These and many other difficulties in the text, and objections of opponents of the primeval Sabbath, are thus far more satisfactorily met than by the explanations we see generally given; and other inferences may be deduced from this change of day to the Jews which may satisfy the minds of many to whom these difficulties are real obstacles to the right solution of this important question.

But if light is thrown on the change of day for the Jews, it sheds still stronger light on the purpose of God in the change from the Jewish to the Christian day of rest. If it is only *a return to the original Sabbath* which was made for man, and of which, as we have seen, man had kept a record as of the sacred charter of his liberty as a child and servant of God, we can easily see the divine purpose in choosing this day. It could be no accident which so ordered the important events at the death and resurrection of Christ, that the latter should occur on the day so generally recognised as a sacred day, three-fourths, if not nine-tenths of the ancient world retaining some record of it. There were many chances, if we may so speak, against that arrangement, by which the day of the passover should happen on a Jewish Sabbath. The day was regulated by the moon, not by the week, so that it might fall on any day of the seven. It would only occur on a Sabbath once in an average of seven years; and if it had happened on any other day than that on which it did fall, the striking coincidence of the death of Christ on the evening on which the paschal lamb was slain, and his resurrection on the morning of the third, would not have occurred on that day which we have traced with such probability, if not certainty, to the creation Sabbath. The wisdom which fixed the "hour" had also arranged the year and day, so that our blessed Lord should rise, not on the Jewish Sabbath, or any other day of the week, but that which we have seen reason to believe commemorated Jehovah's rest at creation,—the same day on which Christ was to "enter into his rest as God did from his." If that Sunday had been only a day of human origin, and derived from an idolatrous worship of the heavenly bodies, we cannot think that God would so have honoured it, when no adequate reason for changing from the Jewish Sabbath, and specially if that had been the old creation Sabbath, can be shewn. The reasons usually given seem to be insufficient, and no inspired authority can be given in support of them.

One instructive argument for the divine purpose in introducing the Egyptian, or, as we would call it, the primeval week by the Roman government, is seen in the fact that our Lord and the apostles not only adopted the Sunday thus brought in, but adopted also the Roman method of calculating the day from *midnight to midnight*. Much nonsense is spoken about the Jewish division, from sunset to sunset being the only one divinely recognised in Scripture. The fact seems to be strangely overlooked that Scripture settles this question conclusively, if men would only carefully study its pages. So long as the true church was confined to the tropics, and time was but imperfectly measured, nor greatly valued, the old mark of the commencement and close of the day was appropriately regulated by the setting sun ; but for a religion designed for all latitudes, and when the day would vary with the changing seasons of the year, it was important that a definite period of time should be fixed for the com-

---

* See Appendix F.

mencement of the sacred hours of the day of rest, as well as
of the busy days of labour, accordingly the Roman method,
which was known and practised at the time of our Lord,
was recognised and adopted.

In the notice of our Lord's resurrection it is mentioned
in such a way as to shew that the first Sabbath of the new
era was from midnight to midnight. We are told expressly
that Jesus rose "early in the morning, while it was yet
dark;" and by Jewish notation that day should have closed
at sunset, as by their reckoning it had begun at sunset preceding. But we find that "the same day at evening" the
Lord appeared to the disciples, and we are told it was still
"the *first* day of the week" (John xx. 19). The word used is
οψια, that generally employed for the later evening or sunset;
and that it was the later evening, and consequently the
beginning of a new day according to the Jews, is, we think,
rendered certain by the fact recorded in Luke xxiv. 29.
There we learn that it was "toward evening" when the
disciples pressed Jesus to spend the night with them at
Emmaus. After they had so pressed him to stop, "for the
day is far spent," they had eaten their evening meal and
walked a distance of about eight miles at least. They had
met with the disciples, and had time to learn of the Lord's
appearance to Peter, and to tell of his conversation with
them, before "Jesus stood in the midst of them." This
must surely have been after sunset, and yet it was still the
"first day of the week." Time must have been measured,
not by Jewish but by the Roman method. This is put
beyond all question by Acts xx., where it is said Paul waited
at Troas seven days, evidently to have a Sabbath with the
converts.

On the first day of the week when the disciples were come
together to break bread, Paul preached unto them, ready to
depart on the morrow, and continued his speech until midnight. From the eleventh verse we learn that the apostle
left at *break of day*. Now if this was the morrow, *i.e.*, our
Monday morning, of the seventh verse, the writer could not
have reckoned by the Jewish dawn of the day, from sunset
to sunset, for in that case the *break of day*, after that night
of privilege and miracle, would have been but the first hour
of light of the *same* day. The morrow would not have come
till the sunset of that day, when the apostle could not have
travelled without spending another night after that on which
we are told they met and brake bread. But the narrative
is most explicit that the apostle left at daybreak after that
same night, and every hour is accounted for from the time
of lighting the lamps till midnight and on till break of day,

"and so he departed." On the Jewish reckoning the narrative is self-contradictory, but reckoning the day by the usual method it is plain and self consistent. Whether they had any meetings during the day time we are not informed. It is probable they had at night, according to custom, met to observe the Lord's Supper, both as being more in harmony with early usage, and to prolong their enjoyment of the apostle's presence. It was still Sabbath until midnight, and then *the morrow* begins; and we see as day appears the loving fellowship is broken up; the sanctity of Sabbath feeling and of Sabbath exercise unbroken by the short hour of the secular day. The practice of the early Church fully confirms the fact of the Roman day having been adopted from apostolic times, and it appears from the example of Christ and Paul that we have the same divine authority and inspired warrant for beginning our Christian Sabbath at midnight, that we have for changing it from the seventh to the first day of the week. As to this change of terms, seventh or last, and now first day of the week, we can only regard them as relative to the Jewish terms, and as a clear and well understood way of designating the day now set apart. The terms are purely relative, and in no way affect the question at issue.

If the day was distinctly known, it matters little whether it be called first or last of the series. Indeed, at the first institution of the Sabbath in Paradise, the day which was seventh to the Creator in respect of His six days' work was the first to Adam and Eve, who were created on the sixth day, and entered appropriately on their new and blessful life in acts of social worship and holy rest, while fresh from their Maker's hand, and with minds and bodies unwearied by the toils of life.

We may still be asked for some *explicit testimony*, that the day we now observe as commemorative of the Lord's resurrection from the dead is really the same day of the week on which Jehovah rested from His work of creation; and the pious worshipper may feel the want of direct Scripture evidence for such an opinion. But in such a case, is direct testimony to be expected? or is such evidence needed? If we were in search of *authority* for keeping one day in seven as sacred, or for observing this day in preference to another, such historic testimony or scriptural warrant might well be demanded. But such are not the subject of inquiry. The command to set apart one day in seven is explicit and admitted, and the particular day has been fixed by our Lord and his apostles, or, as some say, by the Church; and is

D

allowed to be suitable by all parties, independently of any theory on the subject.

Profane history cannot be asked for direct testimony on such a subject. It does not go far enough back, and it is too much bound up with vain fancies, and heathen mythology, and foolish speculations as to the origin of things. While its records of facts, which were incorporated with old customs, or formed a part of their ancient chronology, or were impressed on conscience, or associated with their religious traditions, might be fully relied on, their reasonings about, or deductions from, them may be quite untrustworthy. While no wise man would do more than weigh the historic evidence for or against the facts they record, every judicious student will form his own independent judgment of the validity of any theory they may propound, regarding the origin or import of these facts.

Neither are we entitled to expect any explicit statement in Scripture as to the identity of the Christian and the creation Sabbath. It is sufficient if the opinion we express be found to harmonise with all that we find recorded regarding the Sabbath, and if we find that it is not only in harmony with all it says, but throws light on what would be otherwise obscure or inexplicable, we are not at liberty to demand more.

Again, we may be asked with more show of reason, if there be any references in the fathers of the Christian Church to the identity of the Lord's day and the Paradisiac Sabbath. We have shewn that they recognised its coincidence with the day to which the heathens attached a character of sacredness. But did they regard the day observed by the heathen as of primeval and divine origin?

Even here we are not entitled to look for anything very explicit. It might have been generally understood, and for that very reason not made the subject of discussion or assertion; it might have been assumed as demanding no proof from its being so generally accepted. Any argument from silence on this subject would be as fallacious as the argument from the silence of the Patriarchs, of which so much is made by the opponents of a primeval Sabbath. I do not positively assert that we can now prove that the Fathers recognised the Sunday of the heathen as a divine institution, or a corruption of the original creation Sabbath. It may not have been a subject in regard to which there was any doubt or discussion, and it is generally difficult to discover the current of influences which lead to changes which are universally and harmoniously effective.

The very absence of opposition renders it difficult to discover the causes at work. Like the smoothness of the river, it implies the depth and strength of the current.

In the writings of the fathers, we find expressions which seem to imply a recognition of this identity. They speak of the *eighth* being identical with the *first*, and being the *real seventh.*

Barnabas, speaking of the Jewish Sabbath, says : ' The Sabbaths which ye now keep are not acceptable unto Me, but those which I have made when *resting from all things.* I shall begin the eighth day, that is the beginning of the world, *for which cause we observe the eighth day with gladness, on which also Jesus rose from the dead."* The *resting from all things* seems naturally to refer to the creation rest, and although he uses the *days* of creation as symbolical of the world's duration for a like number of thousand years, it is confirmatory of our view that he makes the rest of the new world, not on the Jewish seventh, but on the *eighth*, which was also the first of the heptade.

Justin Martyr appears, in some passages of his works, to deny that there was any day of rest and worship before Moses. " For," he says, "if there was no need of circumcision before Abraham, nor of the observance of Sabbath keeping, and festivals, and oblations before Moses, neither now is there any need of them." But he cannot mean that there was no sacred day or sacrifices before Moses, or that the former was abolished now, for he repeatedly refers to the practice of the Church in keeping a day of worship. " We all of us assemble together on Sunday, because it is the first day in which God changed darkness and matter, and made the world, *on the same day* also Jesus Christ rose from the dead," so that he connects creation and the Christian Sabbath. He must refer to the Sabbath with its Jewish name and peculiar day, and possibly meant that the patriarchs had not *their* Sabbath on the same day as the Jews. By this reference to the *first* day as the day of the change of matter at creation, and, at the same time, the day consecrated by the Christian Church to worship, as the day of the sun, on which Christ rose from the dead, he confirms our view that the early Church did recognise the Sunday of the heathen as the original sacred day. This seems to be taught by Tertullian, who was a firm supporter of the primeval Sabbath, but says the Jewish Sabbath "was a temporary Sabbath." And again, apparently in reference to the idea of the identity of the creation and the Christian Sabbath, he says, "That very day which was holy from the beginning by his Father's benediction, he made more holy by His own benefaction " (*Adv. Marcion*). To show what day he meant, he says elsewhere, "we give up to rejoicing the day of the sun."

A sentence from Theophilus of Antioch is still more explicit. In Book II. chap. xii., on "the glory of the six days work," he says, of the philosophers and poets among the heathen : " Moreover, concerning the seventh day, which all men acknowledge; but the most know not that what among the Hebrews is called the ' Sabbath,' is translated into Greek the ' seventh ' (ἑβδομας), a name which is adopted by every nation, although they know not the reason of the appellation." When he says the seventh day of the week corresponded to the Jewish Sabbath, he must have known that their *first* day, which was their sacred day, corresponded to our Christian Sabbath. In the eleventh chapter, he had shewn his conviction of the divine origin of the week, by the way in which he quotes Genesis iii. 2, 3. 2ʹ. 2, 3ʹ ?

Clement of Alexandria throws light on the idea the early Church had of creation and the day of rest, referred to by Justin and others, when he says, " The commaudment (the fourth) informs us that the world was made by God, and that He gave us the seventh day for rest, on account of the sufferings and afflictions of life, and the *eighth appears to be rightly called the seventh*, and to be the true seventh."— *Strom.*, Lib. vi. ch. 16,

And again, what does Epiphanius mean, when he says, " The first Sabbath from the beginning decreed and declared by the Lord in the creation of the world, has revolved in its cycle of seven days from that day till now ?" This looks like a clear recognition of the identity of the creation and Christian Sabbath for which we contend.

These, and similar expressions which might be quoted, all favour the idea that the early Church not only knew that the resurrection of Christ sanctioned and sanctified the " Sunday " or " Lord's day," which was known to the heathen world, but that that day, of which the heathen had kept the correct record, was the original Sabbath appointed by God at the beginning, and now rendered doubly sacred by the completion of redemption on the day which closed the work of creation.

The evidence is all that we could reasonably look for in regard to such a change as was made at the transition from the Jewish to the Christian Sabbath. Those who know a little of the writings of the early fathers are aware, that on many more important points, their testimony is very scanty, and, viewed by itself, far from conclusive.

Take, for example, all that can be gathered on the subject of infant baptism, or the *mode* of baptism, and how little do we find in comparison with what we might have expected? and yet, I suppose, it will be considered by disputants on both sides that it is as much as could be looked for in the circumstances, and by all, the comparative silence will be accounted for in the same way. It is, because the view which each advocates "was the *unquestioned* belief and practice of the early Church," we shall be told; "It did not need to be formally stated; it never was a subject of discussion." I not only can bring forward clearer evidence from the "fathers" that the early Christians did recognise the identity of the Christian and the creation Sabbath, than can be adduced on either side of the baptist controversy; but I have a much more conclusive proof, not only for the adoption of the *Lord's day*, but also for the reason of its *universal* and *unquestioned adoption*.

Not only is the *Scripture* evidence sufficient, but the *day was so obviously made for their use and advantage*, by the introduction of the ancient week, with its sacred day, from Egypt into the Roman Empire, that we are constrained to look to an over-ruling Providence preparing the way for the change.

But, apart from all consideration of what the fathers said, or the influences at work on the introduction of the Christian Sabbath, I return to our historic fact, which we are willing to leave, without further comment, to the study of thoughtful and honest minds. It would have been easy to multiply proofs from other sources in favour of a week, and day of sacred observance. For example, I could adduce the names and order of the days of the week in our own Saxon tongue. Any one with a good lexicon may see that our names bring the evidence of both Saxon and Scandinavian tradition to support that of Egpyt and India, and all the nations of Europe, whose language is based on the Latin, such as France, Spain, and Portugal, bring additional weight to the early introduction of the Egypto-Roman week into these countries, apparently before the spread of Christianity. I might have brought evidence from Africa, if the more ancient and authentic record from Egypt had not fully represented the race of Ham. But enough, and more than enough, has been adduced to establish the important truth, that all antiquity bears evidence to the identity of the Christian and creation Sabbath. I do not think it necessary to enlarge on the importance of this testimony to the day which the Lord hath blessed. I attach no superstitious importance to "days, and months, and times, and years," but I do reverence that day which has been consecrated by God from the beginning, and of which He most wonderfully preserved the record in every region of the earth. It is not only a seventh portion of time which God requires, but He has decreed that the earth shall, as one family, observe the same day. Not the same in absolute time, but the same in succession. The first Sabbath sun which dawned on Paradise continued in his course to the west, to illumine the yet unpeopled lands with what was to each quarter of the world its first Sabbath day; and such has been the unbroken chain of Sabbaths, that the sacred seventh day which shed its light on the solitude of our little isle some five or six hours later than on the garden of Eden, has never been lost; and we can say the same of other lands in every degree of longitude, east or west. I dare not trifle with a fact like this,—I dare not tamper with a day to which the finger of God points in the historic consciousness of the world. It seems to bear as clear an evidence for one set and heaven-appointed day of rest and worship as human conscience bears to the one object of worship. I would like to pursue the evidence in favour of a weekly Sabbath from the analogies in nature,—from the physical, intellectual, moral, and spiritual nature of man as an individual, and as a member of society; and I feel assured that, had I the time and talents required for such an investigation, the evidence for our Sabbath would stand forth as unassailable, even by the weapons of unbelief, as the doctrine of the unity of God, as maintained in our better works on natural theology, But I must leave to other and abler hands the elaboration of the evidence for a *Sabbattologia Naturalis.* Enough for my purpose, if I have called attention to the divine intention in preserving the original Sabbath. May He, who at first did institute the day, preserve it from all assaults, and make the diffusion of its blessings as permanent in duration and universal in their compass, as the records of its existence and antiquity.

APPENDIX.

———o———

NOTE A.—P. 12.

Since writing the preceding pages, my attention has been called to an article which appeared in the *Chinese Repository* for March 1849. It is part of a sermon, by a Chinese preacher,—one of Dr Morrison's first converts. In proving to his countrymen that the Sabbath was anciently known in China, he quotes the passages I have given from the classics. As his evidence is both interesting and important, I give a few of his remarks.

After enforcing a seventh day of rest, he says, "But now there are people in many countries entirely ignorant of the Sabbath. This is the cause, men's hearts are continually treacherous, and the heart of rectitude is ever small; so that, the longer the world exists, the more it forgets the commands of God. If we trace the matter up, it will be found that there is now no country which does not know the Sabbath, and even the Chinese speak of it. The diagram, *Fuh*, in the 'Book of Changes,' says, ' this rule goes and returns, *in seven days it comes again.*' Twan (Prince Wan), says, ' This rule, going and returning, and in seven days coming again, refers to the revolutions of heaven.' This is a trace of a seventh day rest coming round; for if not, why did these ancient worthies speak in such a way ? The age of Fuh-hi (from whom the first quotation was made), ' was not far from the creation, and the time of a Sabbath was not yet altogether forgotten in China, and his not saying seven moons, or seven times, but *seven days,* is a clear trace of it. But, unhappily, those who afterwards expounded the Book of Changes, could not at all follow in his steps, and made quite another meaning, which is much to be regretted. In the sentence (also quoted from the Book of Changes,) ' Do we again see the heart of heaven and earth ? ' this is still plainer. The Chinese use the phrase, *heaven and earth,* to indicate the Supreme Ruler, and he instituted the Sabbath, with no other reason than to benefit the bodies and the souls of men, as the Scriptures say, ' the Sabbath was made for man.' Do we not again see, in this, the love of God for man ? Truly these words are trustworthy. In respect of the expression, (continuing to quote from the same book), ' The ancient kings ordered that on that day the gate of the great road should be shut, and traders not permitted to pass, nor the princes to go and examine their states,' it is plainly to be seen, that in the time of the ancient kings, on the day of the Sabbath, all classes kept at rest, and observed it. Is it so, that the Chinese had not at first a Sabbath ? "

These comments, on the most venerated of the Chinese classics, by a native of well known intelligence and honesty, are the more valuable from being the independent result of his own careful study. He had been told, by his first and much-esteemed instructor, that the Chinese had no knowledge of a Sabbath, and this was accounted for on the theory that the Sabbath was not instituted in Paradise, but at some later period, after the founders of the Chinese empire had separated from the rest of mankind. And yet the truth is forced upon him, by his own reflection, that these old records *did* speak of a week and a day of rest.

To explain the enigmatical form of the expressions quoted, I may briefly refer to the book in which they are found. They are all taken from the most ancient and revered of all the sacred books of the Chinese, called the Yih King, or Book of Changes. It was compiled in prison, by Prince Wan, also called Twan, about the year 1150 before the Christian era. This literary prince, as his name imports, found, even at that remote period, certain fragments of great antiquity, attributed on what seems very good authority, to Fuh-hi, who flourished three or four hundred years after the flood, and with whom, according to the generally received opinion of both Chinese and European scholars, the authentic history of China begins. Fuh-hi embodied, or we might rather say concealed, his philosophy in eight diagrams, which were increased to sixty-four. These diagrams have exercised the acutest minds in China for more than three thousand years, and are still a mystery. Along with these figures he lays down a body of rules, or, as they are sometimes called, institutes, and states truths which seem to have been the general belief of that early period.

The expression, " Seven days complete a revolution," as given at p. 11 from memory, is a free but just rendering of one of these old truths, thus traced back to the days of Noah. It is given more literally in the article quoted from the *Repository*, and the editor, in a note, gives it more fully. Fuh-hi, referring to the diagram called *Fuh*, says, " This law goes and returns, in seven days it comes again, wherever it influences advantages follow." The three subsequent quotations are from Prince Wan, who not only compiled, in the 12th century B.C., the earlier work of Fuh-hi, but added important scholia of his own, which are regarded with almost as great veneration as the original. The last of these, if taken as referring to the seventh day, previously spoken of, or *the law* which is said to *go and return in seven days*, is more explicit than as given by me, " on the seventh day the passages are closed," and as I lay no claim to Chinese scholarship, I gladly accept the fuller and more accurate rendering, " *on that day* the gate of the great road should be shut."

That this was by order of the " ancient kings," gives great significance to the fact referred to. Those kings, who were *ancient* in the 12th century, B.C., must, from Chinese notions of antiquity, be such as Fuh-hi and his successors, not long after the flood, and if " traders were not permitted to pass, nor the princes to go and examine their

states," on " that day," we may well ask, with the preacher, " Is it
so, that the Chinese have not a Sabbath ? "

I have no desire to conceal the fact that no heathen Chinese scholar
interprets these passages as the Christian has done, of a week and a
Sabbath. This division of time, as well as the practical observance
of a day of rest, was lost at an early period, along with the true knowledge and worship of God. The decimal system was applied by them
to time as to other things, and, like the Greeks, they have long regulated the recurrence of market days, &c., by decades. The last quotation is doubly instructive, it shows what the ancient kings did on
the seventh day, but it indicates also, that what had been done by
these ancient kings was no longer the custom in his day. And if the
law prescribing a day of rest was disused in the twelfth century, we
need not wonder that it was unknown in the sixth century B.C.,
when Confucius restored the book, which had been in a great measure
lost to the nation. Many European students of Chinese literature
also try to explain away these passages. Starting with the general
assumption that there is no trace of a Sabbath in China, they are as
much lost in their vain guesses at the meaning of these passages as
the Chinese themselves. On our interpretation of these passages,
they are naturally and comparatively easily understood, and we fairly
challenge any scholar, either native or foreign, to explain them
consistently in any other way. There are 1450 treatises on that Book
of Changes in the catalogue of the imperial library alone, how many
there are in China no man can tell. Not one of them satisfies an independent student, and the same may be said of any attempt by
Europeans. Is it not by refusing the explanation furnished by
Moses in the second chapter of Genesis? These passages in the
classics would never of themselves lead us to suppose that the Chinese
had once a knowledge of the septenary division of time. But let
these passages be viewed in the light of the proofs we give in the
other facts or classes of facts at pp.10–12, and our interpretation of
them will appear the natural, if not the inevitable, one. These facts
put any one, who reads and understands their import, in about as
good a position for understanding these passages as the Chinese
scholar; better than those who start with a wrong assumption.

Note B. —P. 13.

I find that I have greatly understated the evidence from Indian
history in regard to the record of a week of seven days, and a Sunday
corresponding to that of the western nations. This record is found
in the most ancient of their literature, the Sanscrit, and the attempts
which are made to account for its introduction by the opponents of
the divine origin of this division of time, only shew the shifts to
which men are put by the adoption of a false theory. Dr Hessey
thinks it may be accounted for by "the intercourse of the Jews with
Egypt, and the expeditions of Egyptian conquerors into Scythia,
which, according to Sir Henry Rawlinson, was the cradle of the Per-

sians and 'Hindoos,' while others refer its introduction to the Arabs and Mohamedans."

How Egyptian expeditions could have such a result is difficult to conceive. If the Egyptians had kept the infant nation of Persia and Hindostan in subjection for a length of time, and moulded their institutions when they were in their cradle in Scythia, it might have been possible to transfer the week from Egypt to India. But an *Expedition of Conquerors* is not likely to inspire infant nations with a love for their institutions. Especially, when these are not evidently fitted to promote material prosperity, and less likely when connected with religious ideas.

But the supposition is an evident anachronism. The intercourse of the Jews with the Egyptians, spoken of by Dr Hessey, must have been at a period long subsequent to the emigration of the Hindoos from Central Asia, and that the Indian week was not copied from the Mohamedans, is proved from the well known fact, that they entirely differ from each other. The most sacred day of the Mohamedan week, is on our Friday ; that of the Hindoos, is on our Sunday. Besides, the names do not so resemble as to imply a derivation the one from the other ; and, moreover, the week, with the Sanscrit names, was transferred to the Hindoo colony in Bali, long before the birth of Mohamed.

The following interesting Table, shewing the identity of the order and names of the days of the week in India with those of Europe, is taken from an able article in the *British and Foreign Evangelical Review* for April 1866.

Sanscrit days of the week, as yet scarcely changed in India.	Names at length introduced into Rome.	English names (with the meanings in all the three languages).
Aditya-war.	Dies-Solis.	Sunday, or day of the Sun.
Soma-war.	Dies-Lunæ.	Monday, or day of the Moon.
Mangala-war.	Dies Martis.	Tuesday, or day of Mars.
Buddha-war.	Dies-Mercurii.	Wednesday, doubtfully identified with Mercury.
Brahaspat-war.	Dies-Jovis.	Thursday, or day of Jupiter.
Sucra-war.	Dies-Veneris.	Friday, or day of Venus.
Shun-war.	Dies-Saturni.	Saturday, or day of Saturn.

" Here" the writer adds, "is an uncommonly curious and interesting series of facts. Not merely is there a division into weeks in various lands, the several days being named after the sun, moon, and planets, but making allowance for difference of longitude, the Sunday of any one country has, it would appear, always fallen on precisely the same day with the Sunday of all others, and so with the remaining days of the week."

In a note, kindly sent me, in answer to some inquiries regarding the above table, the writer of the article says, " The Indian Aditivar (Sunday), and the Sabbath of Europe, are to all intents and purposes *on the same* DAY, the only difference is one of HOURS, that is, that when it is noon here, it will be about five in the afternoon in India, owing to the difference of longitude."

In connection with the above table, we subjoin one taken from a valuable note on Dion Cassius, by Reimarus. We leave out the names of the planets in Arabic and Persic, as they are imperfectly given in Hebrew characters, from which little can be learned, we give only the Egyptian, which he represents in Greek character, the Hebrew, Jewish, and the Grecian, along with the signs for the planets, which have been transmitted from the earliest times to the science of the present day, and to these we have added the more recent names in Greece and Italy.

Signs.	Roman Names.	Egyptian.	Hebrew Names.	Hebrew Names in Greek Characters, from Epiphanius.	Greek.
☉	Sol	Πιρη	חמה or שמש	Ημα και Σεμις	ʿΗλιος
☽	Luna	Πιιος	לבנה	Ιιρι και Αλβανα	Σιληνη
♂	Mars	Μολοχ	מאדים	Χωχιβ, Οχμωλ	Αρης
☿	Mercurius	Πιερμης	כוכב	Χωχιβ, Οχμοδ	ʿΕρμης
♃	Jupiter	Πιξιυς	צדק	Χωχιβ, Βααλ	Ζιυς
♀	Venus	Σουροτ	נוגה	Σεροδα	ʾΑφροδιτη
♄	Saturnus	Ρηφαι	שבתאי	Χωχιβ Σαβηθ	Κρόνος

We have taken the liberty of altering this table, as well as of omitting and adding to it, but not without a careful reference to the authorities from which it is professedly taken. Ρηφαν, or Saturn, he puts first, without giving any reason for doing so. Epiphanius and Bede both put it *last*. Epiphanius (Κατα φαρισαιων), treating of the superstition of the Jews, gives them in the order we have observed, putting the sun first, and ending with "lastly," *Saturn* is called Χωχεβ Σαβηθ. In the Latin version the translator renders it " Saturnus *denique* cochab Sabeth vocatur."

Bede gives three arrangements in the order of the names. In a chapter entitled, " Ordo Planetarum juxta naturam et numerum earum secundum Hebraeos," he says, " Sol qui dicitur juxta Hebraeos Hama, prima est Planetarum, Secunda Venus, quæ dicitur Noga, Tertia Mercurius, id est cocaph ; Quarta Luna, quæ et Libala, Quinta Saturnus, videlicit Sabbai, Sexta Jupiter, id est Sedech, Septima Mars qui et Madei," &c.

In another chapter, " De Ratione," he gives a different order from any we have met with, beginning with Saturn, the Sun fourth, and the Moon last. And in a third chapter of his Prognostica, " De Septem Feriis," which alone has reference to the order of days of the week, the order is as we have given it above, only for the first and last he has the names of Lord's day and Sabbath. " Dominus," being an old heathen designation for the sun, and it is interesting to find the Hebrew name for the seventh day used to designate Saturn, and identified with the same planet as called by the Egyptians Ρηφαν

(Rephan), which, according to Stephen, was the first, or one of the first, objects of Sabian idolatry after the departure from Egypt (Acts vii. 43). " The star of your god Remphan," or more properly, Rephan. This throws important light on the question of the origin of the names of the week, and seems to prove that the names of the seven days were not derived from the planets, but that the names of the days set apart for the worship of particular deities *were transferred to the planets*, which were the seats or symbols of these gods, *not that the name of the planet was transferred to the day*. It is admitted on all hands, that the name *Sabbath* was divinely appointed as the designation of the Jewish day of worship. We find that the Jews, departing from the worship of Jehovah, gave the name of their sacred day to the planet Saturn, and if the Jews at an early period took this way of giving names to the planets and gods, *is it not extremely probable, if not certain, that they did so* after the customs of their heathen neighbours ? This probability is greatly strengthened by the fact, that the planet which they designated שבתאי (Sabbathai), or, according to Epiphanius Σαβηθ (Sabbath), or as Bede spells it, Sabbai, was called by the Egyptians Rephan, and stands in their arrangements of the days of the week *on the same day as the Jewish Sabbath*, and, as will be seen from our two tables, occupies the same place in the week of other lands.

NOTE C.— P. 15.

' In Book lxvii. ch. 7, he says, " Οὕτω μὲν τὰ Ἱεροσόλυμα ἐν αὐτῇ τῇ τοῦ χρόνου ἡμέρᾳ, ἣν μάλιστα ἔτι καὶ νῦν Ἰουδαῖοι σεβουσιν, ἐξώλετο." " Thus Jerusalem, on that very day of Saturn, which day chiefly the Jews then and now reverence, was utterly destroyed."

Again, in Book xxxvii. ch. 16, referring to the taking of the temple after the capture of the city, he says, " Nor if they had defended it equally every day (or on all the days) would it have been taken, but because on Saturn's day (Saturday), as the day is called, they refrained from fighting," &c, " νῦν δε τας τοῦ χρόνου δὴ ὠνομασομένας ἡμέρας διαλείποντες," &c.

This has all the appearance of being an account of the destruction of the city, and of the cause of the failure of the Jews in defending it, taken from some contemporary narrative now lost to us. And it is specially worthy of note, that the writer speaks of the days of the week entirely from a heathen point of view, as if they were familiarly known at that early period by Roman or Greek writers. He could not be speaking of the Jewish week, or he would never have spoken of the Jews calling their sacred Sabbath after the name of the heathen deity Saturn. The Jewish name of the planet Saturn in Greek was, as we have seen, Σαβηθ. And as little can we suppose that he was using the language of Christians. It is true that we find the Christian apologist using the same names for the days of the week. But that was because their names were known to the heathens. As for example, Justin Martyr (born about 112), in his address to the Emperor Antoninus Pius, calls the Christian day of worship Sunday. ." They met τῇ τοῦ

'Ηλίου λεγομένη ἡμέρα." And in his dialogue with Trypho, he tells us that our Lord was crucified on a Saturday, and rose on a Sunday the day after Saturday, " ἥ μετὰ τὴν κρονικὴν ἥτις ἐστὶν ἡ τοῦ 'Ηλίου ἡμέρα."

We can only account for this use of the heathen names for the days of the week by both Christian and heathen writers, from these being the names in familiar use at that early period. And we feel fully justified in maintaining that the week, as found in Egypt, was introduced into the Roman empire at or before the commencement of the Christian era, probably in the year 46 B.o., when the calendar was reformed, and that, while it was adopted by the Romans from its obvious antiquity and accuracy, the change was providentially arranged by God for the preparing of the way for the introduction of the Christian religion and specially of its day of sacred rest.

I have not adduced any of the oft quoted passages from ancient, Greek and Latin authors, to shew that the Greeks and Romans had, at an early period of their history, a trace of the week of seven days, not because I think such a trace cannot be found, even as far back as the days of Homer, but because I do not attach much importance to the evidence, even if more clear than it is. I think too much has been attempted to be proved from the passages quoted. The most that can be directly proved from such passages as are collected by Eusebius and others, and repeated in many of the Puritan and modern writers, is, that there was *somethiny sacred in the number seven*, and that this sacredness applied *to the seventh period of time*, as to the seventh day of the month, the seventh month. And I agree with Dr S. Lee, in thinking that neither Aristobulus, Clemens, nor Eusebius, quoted sayings from the ancients to establish a regular recurring seventh sacred day, but only a certain sacredness in a seventh period of time.

That other days were sacred does not destroy this evidence. In the Christian Church there are saints' days as well as Sabbaths. Let any one look over the reference to sacred days, and he will be struck with the vast preponderance of evidence for the sacredness of the seventh, which is a shadowy kind of proof in favour of a tradition of an early observance of a week even in Greece.

I have seen it stated, though I cannot now remember where, that the Greeks have a tradition that time was once measured by seven days, and that it was afterwards changed into decades. This is such a change as was likely to be made by such a people, more under the control of rationalism than religion, or superstition, in their later history, like the French, at the Revolution, when they made a like change on the week. The same change from seven to ten has been made in China from a remote period. While time for practical purposes in China has been divided into decades for many centuries, they have still left the record of an earlier division by sevens, more clear and definite than can now be found in the extant writings of ancient Greek authors. Yet even in the latter, the evidence for a sacred seven is not to be lightly set aside. I can see no sufficient reason for rejecting all the quotations from Hesiod and Homer, which are not found in their works as we now have them. They are allowed to be incomplete. As for Callimachus and Linus, from whom also interesting quotations are given, we possess but a few poems of the former, who is reported to have written eight hundred works ; and though the latter is little better than a mythical person, still the verses attributed to him may have been genuine specimens of antiquity.

For the evidence from Roman writers, as well as Grecian, we must refer to accessible works like Owen on " Hebrews," or Gale's " Court of the Gentiles," &c. I attach little importance to either. Both countries showed their sense of the superiority of the chronology of Egypt as soon as they understood it, by rejecting their own in its favour. I have not thought it necessary to quote authorities for the antiquity of the Egyptian week. It is universally admitted.

Note D.—P. 19.

It strongly confirms the opinion formerly expressed, that the derivation of the names of the days of the week was only a later fancy of the Greeks and Romans, when we compare the fact brought forward in the preceding note, with the well known tendency of the ancient philosophers to attribute effects to most inadequate causes, and often to mistake a coincidence for a cause. Dion Cassius himself gives the theory of the derivation of the seven sounds in music, from the seven planets. An opinion held by eminent philosophers, and expressed in verse by the learned Varro, thus—

" Videt et ætherio mundum torquerier axe
  Et septem æternis sonitum dare vocibus orbes,
  Nitentes aliis quæ maxima divis,
  Laetitia stat tunc longe gratissima Phœbi,
  Dextera consimiles meditatur reddere voces."

But there is another aspect of the connection of the seven days of the week with the seven planets which it pleased the Creator to render visible to the naked eye. May it not have been the design of Him who set the sun and moon "for signs and for seasons, and for days and years," to perpetuate, among all nations the observance of the seven-day-week, by the silent testimony of the seven witnesses in heaven. We cannot fathom the Divine purposes, but we see that the design of God to preserve this septenary division of time, has been attained, in its association with the seven planets, in almost all parts of the world. That God attaches great importance to this division, and to the one sacred day which it was designed to conserve, is seen from its prominence in the institutions of Moses and of Christ, even if we denied its institution at the creation, and the witness of the seven planets, the seven sounds in the scale of music, and the seven colours in the rainbow, would teach the early world that this *sacred seven*, which they found in the diverse regions of space and time, which met the eye in the hues of heaven and earth, and touched the ear with such varied, and yet simple and harmonious sounds, implies *a unity of plan in the natural and moral arrangements of the Divine Ruler ;* and the analogies in nature would dispose men more readily to acquiesce in His arrangements for observing a day of stated rest and worship in every week, and even when they neglected religious duty, to remember and perpetuate the record of its institution. We have no doubt the seven planets preserved the week, amid the heathenism of the world, until the time arrived for its restoration to its original design.

Note E. P.—25.

The change of the day at the departure from Egypt, and the restoration of the original day of rest, as observed from the creation, and restored at the resurrection, will be rendered clearer by the following plan :—

Creation Week.	Order of days as observed by heathen.	Days of the month Ex.xiv.	Jewish week.
6th,	Saturday,	15th,	Day of march from Elim to Sin.
7th,	Sabbath,	16th,	1st Day of Fall of Manna.
1st,	Monday,	17th,	2d,
2nd,	Tuesday,	18th,	3d, ...
3d,	Wednesday,	19th,	4th, ...
4th,	Thursday,	20th,	5th, ...
5th,	Friday,	21st,	6th, ...
6th,	Saturday,	22d,	7th, Manna ceased, now made the Sabbath of the Jews.
7th,	Sabbath,	23d,	1st day of Jewish week, on which Christ rose, and thus restored the *primitive* Sabbath.

If the above be compared with the tables at p. 38, the coincidence will be found very striking. It will be seen that the sacred day of the Jews was different from that of all other people, from India (we may say from China) to the west of Europe. The only exception I know of, is that of the Syro-Phenicians who, according to Porphyry, as quoted by Eusebius, " kept the seventh as well as the Jews." This one exception only confirms the general rule, as we knew that *Saturn* was their god, and was worshipped on *Saturday*, which was also the day of Saturn, or Rephan in the Egyptian week. Was not this the occasion of the Israelites so frequently falling into the worship of that god? If their day of rest was Saturday, it was natural, when they departed from the true God, that they should adopt the god worshipped by their idolatrous neighbours the Egyptians and the Syro-Phenicians, on that day, as Stephen tells us, they were *in the habit* of doing. See the use of the imperfect tense in Acts vii. 43.

I cannot here give anything like even a *resumé* of the argument for such a change as, we suppose, took place at the exodus. I only refer to it as lying in the way of our argument, not as necessary to its validity. Those who wish to see the question discussed at length, can find it ably argued in " a sermon by Dr Samuel Lee, preached before the University of Cambridge, on Sunday, June 30th, 1833." I regret that I did not see it until this pamphlet was in type. Many of the ablest and soundest writers of the seventeenth and eighteenth centuries held the same views.

But while many passages of Scripture seem to imply such a change, and to anticipate a return to the original Sabbath, it is not of importance for us to press the theory, however probable it may appear. The coincidence of the resurrection of Christ on the first day of the Jewish week, can be accounted for without supposing that the day was changed by Divine appointment, at the departure from Egypt. Amongst other ways of accounting for it, that of an error having crept into the later reckoning of the Jewish week may be suggested. They may have lost a day, and thus transferred the Sabbath from the seventh to the sixth day of the week.

During the repeated periods of defection from the worship of Jehovah, which are always characterised by a neglect of the Sabbath, or when dispersed in other countries, that the land of their fathers " might enjoy her Sabbaths," they may have failed to keep a true record of the sacred day. God complains, " Her priests . . . . have hid their eyes from my Sabbaths," * and in righteous judgment he may have fulfilled literally that word, " The Lord hath caused the solemn feasts *and Sabbaths to be forgotten.*" † The probability of such an error having been made, and allowed by God, for the purposes He had in view, is strengthened by the generally-admitted fact, that our Lord kept the passover on the day before that on which it was observed by the Jews, and thus so ordered the grand events of His death and resurrection, that the former should take place on the eve of the slaying of the Paschal Lamb, and the latter on the morning of the primitive Sabbath.

If the Jews had lost their Sabbath before, or during their dispersions, they would be very apt to resume it on the sixth day of the week. They would find the sacred day among the heathen called the *first* day of the week, and not knowing that it was really the seventh, though called first, they would naturally put their Sabbath a day before it, supposing *that* the seventh, though really the sixth of the creation week, as may be seen from the preceding table.

---

* Ezekiel xxii. 26. † Lam. ii. 6.